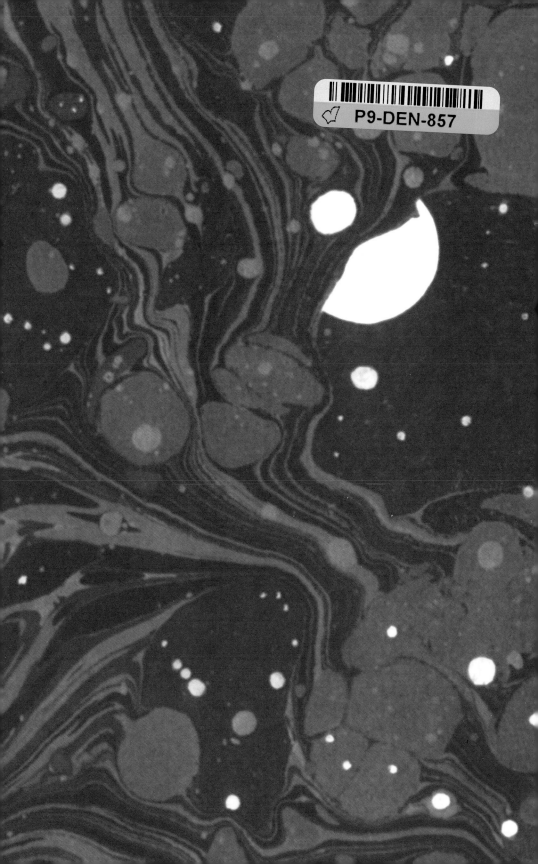

TWO VOICES AND A MOON

TWO VOICES AND A MOON

NEW AND SELECTED POEMS
by
NANCY PRICE

A Malmarie Press Book
Kissimmee, Florida

First Printing

Malmarie Press and colophon are registered trademarks of
Malmarie Press, Inc.

ISBN: 1-934478-11-3
Library of Congress Control Number: 2007908212
First Malmarie Press hardcover printing October 2007
Illustrated by the author

For universities, colleges, schools and organizations: Quantity discounts are
available on bulk purchases of this book for educational use, gift purchases, or as
premiums for increasing magazine subscriptions and renewals. Please contact
Malmarie Press, Inc., 1301 Hidden Harbor Lane, Kissimmee, Florida 34746.
E-mail: nancypricebooks@aol.com   Website: nancypricebooks.com

ALSO BY NANCY PRICE

NOVELS

A NATURAL DEATH
AN ACCOMPLISHED WOMAN
SLEEPING WITH THE ENEMY
NIGHT WOMAN
NO ONE KNOWS
BONFIRE'S DAUGHTER
(in French)
TWO LIARS AND A BRIDE
(in French)

These poems are for my children,
Catherine, John and David,
who were there for me.

My thanks to the editors of many publications
who chose to print most of the poems in this book.
Among them were:

*America, The Atlantic, Audience,
The Blue Guitar, The Colorado Quarterly,
Commonweal, Harper's Bazaar, Kansas Quarterly,
Kayak, The Nation, The New York Times,
Poetry Northwest, Quarterly Review of Literature,
Saturday Review, and Shenandoah.*

This book was advanced by a grant from
The National Endowment for the Arts,
and by residencies at the Tyrone Guthrie
Centre, the Karolyi Foundation, and the
Rockfeller Foundation Bellagio Study
and Conference Center.

TO MY READER

The first voice of this book is your voice,
recreating the poems as you read them. The
second voice is mine. The moon completes
our trio, standing for our surroundings that
sometimes...sometimes...can seem to have
an ear for us, to be coupled with us, though
we are so sure that trees are planted deep
and deaf, and the moon is a stone.

CONTENTS

-I- TWO VOICES AND A MOON

-II- NIGHT COUPLED WITH MUSIC

-III- PULLED BY THAT FULL SONG

-IV- ON NIGHTS LIKE THESE

-V- THE PATH OF AN OLD AIR

-VI- CONTEXTS

-I-

TWO VOICES AND A MOON

TWO VOICES AND A MOON

"Summer nights have no ear for music. Leider
leaves the moon alone, and the night trees."
"But who seems sobbing in slow water
tide beat?"
     "Even on nights like these
the moon is only a stone. Trees are planted
deep and deaf. See how the ocean sleeps
through music. This is the truth, granted?"
"But what trick keeps
night coupled with music? Waves are breaking
pulled by that full song. What rises there
white with grief?"
     "Only a voice taking
cloud by cloud the path of an old air."

HACKBERRY

Bark sags in folds from the crotches down
to where the roots begin secretly, deliberately
to suck water out from under the lawn.
Children know how the knotholes seem to shift
sometimes. (Do gnarled sockets darken
when we walk between it and the young pear?)
Our living room is dark. We wish the tree weren't there.

It's alive with ants. Brisk birds creep
upside down on its hide all day, grooming.
Twenty feet up, squirrels, grubs, beetles
hang with thick shade over us, a ceiling
(tiny breaths, droppings). One dead limb creaks
just over our bench. Wasps dive
sizzling from it. Green leaves fall near us. It's alive.

It never seems to sleep. We hear how it tests
its tether out there, restlessly. All night long
it rubs against the roof. We think it remembers
old years before we were born.
It's killing the grass.
We talk in bed about chain saws, ropes, danger. We take
care not to be heard: it's awake.

LANDMARK

A water tower to stand
for monumental thirst
straddles our graveyard,
bears the town's name and
brims with iron-red hard
water, a toast held up
to common things we die
without. Across the flat land
we see that landmark first
when we turn homeward, come to lie
down under that lifted cup.

MAPLE FOOLS, MISER OAKS

Maple trees cannot wait. They turn first
before frost, prodigal, unrehearsed,
holding no leaves back when the night cold
comes promising winter. They are gold
when oak lamps have only begun to burn.

Oaks hoard, dole out their russet, turn
only at winter's touch. In the hard frost
when maples darken, shiver, their light lost
on every wind, autumn is carpeted
with fool's gold, but the miser oaks burn red.

DAY LILY

The lily keeps honey in her wide-lipped well;
bees let themselves down, heavy and eager,
and sway with her on her stalk.

When they climb out, they are pollen-yellow;
before dark, each in its narrow cell
rubs down its bright black fur.

Down in the lily, white is gold now;
folding, the great wet bell
wrings herself closed in the last light.

IN THE WATER WORLD

In the water world when a fish swims not quite plumb
his fish bowl friends are first to notice the way
he is listing. They tail him to give him some
friendly nips, follow him around and around. Some day
you may miss him, then notice that he has come
sidewise or bottom-up to the brim
of his water world, turning a slow gray
and watching you with little black spots that swim
under glass like puzzle games children play.
Until the game is up, friends stay away.
But when he drifts back, shimmering and dim,
they come around, solicitous, and eat him.

THE CARDINALS

When winter branches black in the forked shapes
pain takes, and fears you have sheltered from
whiten your most desolate landscapes,
sometimes the wintering cardinals come.
They are birds bright as the fiery shapes of need
answered. Wings honed on the stone skies
flash in a black thicket, drifts bleed
with a red sharp as their cries,
and desolation becomes a foil, a frame
for cardinals. Only a fool asks whether
black and white kindle each bird to flame,
or how fire is struck from such iron weather.

INTERSECTION

Red light. He stops and starts to swear and fidget,
but she's another breed: she idles back
to stare at paving stones like coffin lids
lying in wait for judgment day to crack
and let the dead crawl from the chrysalis
wizened and newly fleshed. Like Mackinac,
Manhattan will be red with Indians
that green light day. It always makes her shiver
to think of Romans marching into Rome
along the Appian Way, a dusty river
of untombed heathens, saints uncatacombed,
while from the Ganges some celestial siever
hauls up the dark-eyed dead, and drowned men come
arrowing out of the ocean's quiver.
All Asia harvested like golden grain,
and Africa brought in as black as oil:
a gush of gleaming bodies come again
to crowd the earth, finger familiar soil,
fill up the homesick eye with sky again.
Out of the maw of death perhaps she'll stroll
this street with him and reminisce Manhattan—
Green light. Their car leaps on the paving stones,
and she's aware the light's still red for bones.

KEEPSAKE

Two young men smile from their tintype space
where a lamp on the table glows.
Opposite, alone in her shadowy place,
sits a girl. No one in the family knows

who they were. Once they were close kin,
but a haze pushes them farther back each year
as their pictured air darkens. We look in
to find their faces smooth, their eyes clear

of any doubt: who could forget their names?
Their collars are so white, their backs straight.
Sure of us, they pose in their narrow frames.
Every night their lamp burns late.

We keep them for the sake of the old leather
case: it folds in your lightest grasp
to shut the smiling faces up together
under a blackened silver hasp.

PASSING THROUGH

We may seem to take winter lying down
here among abandoned gardens, mole-deep,
dull as toads, blown, an occasional leaf,
beneath emptied trees, but a hot word
pulls us up, snowblind yet quivering. Haven't you
halted at least once with drawn breath,
stopped in your track before dark to see
gardens, gas pumps, chimneys, trash cans, the world
climbing upward through winter, the clotted,
the bitter and heavy, the down-falling
snow? All things then, even the trees, are leaving.

SLIPPAGE
For David

An hour ago the creek caught
morning, October, the eleven-year-old, and me
in its mirror, cloudy as agate.
Maples are red there
  yet, a leaf slipping, now and then, from their full arms.

What time is it, time for school
now? Late. The creek flows on. Late.
The woods gate is half closed.
Elderberries are beaded there
  yet. A black berry, now and then, slips a red thread.

Cold, fresh as water on stones,
a marigold's pale spider, a pendulum
hung from her picked flower, is shut in a jar now.
The child is young
  yet, under the school clock's slipping hand.

The smell of marigolds, the taste of berries.
Milk has not dried here on the lip of a glass.
The mail has not even come.
But the spider, on her snapped flower
  yet, is reaching out, groping in air. She feels for

  what's slipped out of reach, barely gone.

-II-

NIGHT COUPLED WITH MUSIC

IN THIS SAME COUNTRY

And there are, in this same country,
angels. They light in a startled hour,
crying joy. How many times our fields
ring with them, grass blade and branch and flower.
Sheep graze, but we see the world clear
as a sweetly-running stream. High cries warn
the dog. He stirs, barks, but he never knows
something is born.
We are sore afraid, yet we listen. One among us
plays that joy back on his lonely horn.

HOW DO YOU TELL
AN ARROWHEAD FROM A STONE?

By the way rock
takes on meaning. Not much.
Enough to bind a shaft to.

Arrowheads are stone, mostly,
but a glint of light, an edge
always runs to a point along the grain

until you feel as much as see
a wedge of flint like a poem,
rough-cut to go straight.

THE TEN-TOED SIGNATURE

Briny, wrapped in the toweling wind and sun,
she runs along the seaweed track alone
where seas trowel back, trowel back,

                             foaming and black,
smoothing a pavement for her signature
in delicate ten-toed pentameter.
Sniggering seas slip back, fawning and slack,
laying a carpet for her with an air
obsequious, a carpet to nowhere
she knows. She isn't fooled. Behind her back
seas pull the rug out, pull the past out, pull
the footprints out. She walks the crumbling floor
between false waters and the fickle shore.

FIREWORKS
To a poet

Darkness that detonates, star hung on star,
rockets livid as truth that will transfix
night with the light that shows us where we are—
these are the fires we work with, green-man tricks
dreamed up by gunners. Learn your pyrotechnics;

ask: Where's the saltpeter word, the primers
fusing the quick-matched phrases? Dynamite
shudders set off the poet from the rhymers,
and incandescent, phosphorescent light
lovers shed in the intermittent night

lit by their own combustion. Find the spark
that blasts off, climbing the midnight stair
free of words, trembling above the dark.
A great one goes on bursting upon the air,
and any time you look it burns there.

ONE-NIGHT FAIR

A traveling fair pitched by our pasture gate
once. I still remember the ferris wheel's
yellow lights turning upon the dark
like a slow mill, only it spilled a freight
of music-run, not water, and girls' squeals
from bucket seats. We rode that contraption late
and long as our nickels lasted. Like a lark
you rode that thing up to the music, hung
over our barn lot, pig pens, then you froze
cleaving your way back down, a dead weight,
to fields you'd spent the years of your life among
and never seen before. It was one of those
one-night fairs, gone as quick as it came
with only trampled grass when the sun rose
to prove where it was. I found out the way it feels
high up there, saw how the home place goes
turning under the night. There's no right name
for a sight like that. The farm's never looked the same.

MERRY-GO-ROUND

A glitter turns against the black
flood of the river, night trees
my children ride away, ride back,
fixed in their course, a zodiac
whirled to the music's shriek and wheeze
a glitter turns against the black
I frame them whole, caught in a crack
between my hands, a captured frieze
my children ride away, ride back
caught in my dark, my black Kodak
that will not lose the thing it sees
my children ride away, ride back
against the black to come, a lack
of any light but nights like these
a glitter turns against the black
my children ride away, ride back.

BASKET

Not machines, but dripping hands stripped willow,
gripped it underfoot, splayed up the split,
wet, whipping rods to a dreamed-of shape
with no false twist, not one, in a pattern older
than cloth. Osier writhed in a round rim
tough as muscle fiber, and locked, dried.
    Willow takes light now.
    Light takes willow.
    They wreathe in a circle round air,
    a delicate measure
    ringing-in silence, and holding.

A DO-IT-YOURSELF POEM

In Colorado once, Iowans,
farm-hungry, scooped up that western dirt
in their calloused hands. It was crumbling
                         and richly black.
They staked claim, out-waited the winter,
waited out the summer, and almost starved.

They had the seed. They had the plows
                         and the prayers
and the babies coming, yes, and the strong arms
and the willing backs. What were they waiting for?
Rain. That was all. And it never came,
and never would. Now you go on, like they did:

say, "That's life."
Make your own metaphor.

BREAKERS

Thundering in between
tide and tide, luminous waters crack
beached rock, splinter the floating green
boughs of trees, smash them back
on shore, battered and dripping. Yet the thin
scallops and china urchins, riding a bland
froth, may be carried so gently in.
Coral branches flower upon this sand
whole. With a sound I have heard before
the waves rise blind, walk in their sleep,
talking to themselves along the dark shore,
wondering what to break, wondering what to keep.

NASSAU: THE DIVERS

In sea churned green from blue,
in light like gilt foil
black divers swim with our ship, break through
orange peels, patches of oil slick,
their faces lift to us, grin, drip,
drag a hot mesh of sun glitter
over limbs under water. They shout:
"Quarta! Dive for quarta!"
   In a straggling row
boys elbow, shove, titter,
beg money as our ship moves past the dock, go
scrambling after a dime. A foot kicks out,
and the smallest gives up his coin to squat
folded in pain, face set.
   But the divers, hand over hand,
take the sheer ship side, climb to us, taut
under water streams. They print wet tracks
among deck chairs, stand
hard-muscled, glistening.
   Our long shadow,
a twilight falling on sheds and ships, advances
to a child on the last wharf playing in wood chips.
We toss down nickels and dimes, but he doesn't know
where such a shower comes from: dazzled, he dances
in jingling silver. The cool of our shadow slips
over, leaves him there on the sunny quay,
happy as divers falling back in an arc,
mouths crammed with money,
dark arms full of the sea.

NASSAU: BY THE DOCKS

Harbor women lounge in chattering rows,
weaving straw in the shade. Children wade
and cry round them like gulls. When a man throws
a glance, they laze, unafraid,
in the backwash of it. They ride
easy on that tide.

Freighters, nose to tail, are warped in
to sag amidships, let the hungry cranes
rummage below. Yawning, they keep up a tin
chatter with old rains,
or lie rusting through noon, lazily
flaking their paint into the sea.

-III-

PULLED BY THAT FULL SONG

OUT OF LOVE: THE BREAK

Cool at last, she has no fever
to make trees waver over
her as if she were a fire; no gardens wilt
into her arms. Once she felt
sun lie hot on her skin,
and a whole clover field crowd in,
fresh and common as desire.
Now every tree is still as a church spire.
Gardens are only flowers. Ripe clover
flushes pink and white, sways over
to nothing but the wind passing. Sun,
touching her, does not feel like anyone.

SOURSOP

Who named them Dock, Dodder,
Corpse-plant, Clammyweed,
Toadflax, Fat-bellies, Horned Bladder-
wort, Spotted Cowbane, Tickseed,
Greasewood, Hairy Vetch, Stonecrop?
Lovers, found flowering innocently, are given such
names with a vengeance, but who envied Soursop
that much?

CORNERED EYE

By sidewise light in the eye's crook
something shimmered like thin ice.
A flicked lash showed her a forked look
like a precipice.

She nearly saw how it waits in him.
She barely sensed how the danger lies
coiled somewhere on the narrow rim
of his half-shut eyes.

Though she is frozen too cold to cry,
too charmed for battle, too fond for flight,
she mounts her guard in a cornered eye
in a sidewise light.

OTHELLO

Iago never betrayed. Self-doubt alone
turned my face to the mirror. Old, black,
I mocked reflection: Why should she be true?
Then Desdemona screamed. The play was done
that moment, and the rest is only lines
spoken by rote under the prompter's cue.
Between my hands her sentenced beauty shines,
the savage spotlights prowl upon my track,
the pages turn, and there's no turning back.

THE DOWAGERS D'ORO

Aging Venetian palaces
take sun along the Grand Canal,
old ladies faintly scandalous
in gemmed ogival necklaces.
Too wise to publish their memoirs,
retired from ball and bacchanal,
they bask in Adriatic wealth
of merchants, doges, emperors,
and try to guard their corridors
from Neptune's old, familiar stealth.
Immortal, mumbling to himself,
all night he tries their crumbling doors.

ECLIPSE OF THE SUN

The sun's circular spangles sign his own
solitary name on grass.
Bodies in space move alone.
But sometimes, down their silent corridors
sun and moon pass
close enough for eclipse. Day blurs,
the sun bows in his place, the moon lies
dark on him from afar;
sparks fly, each like a scimitar
flashing through clouds and leaves to brand shade
with half-suns, dazzles the moon has made
from sunlight curved to a shape of hers.
Dappled, we dare not look: we recognize
such darkly-fused, quivering signatures.

GUITAR

Boy on a park bench, clenched
over your black guitar,
pluck out your taut chords.

Though she laughs, flattens
her young self on air, swinging
off with a chain's cold creak,

trees thrust out sticky buds,
mud, thawing, catches her
flight in its broad pools, and

your big guitar case in
melting snow near her is
open, is lined in red.

HOME MOVIE

Just for laughs, run us all backward now,
shrink the children into my arms, spin
fallen leaves up to the startled bough.
The dead reel back where we two grin
newly-wed in over-exposed glare
until the shutter sticks, and I'm not there.

Drawn backward, caught in the click-click
time makes, slowly reversing sound,
I'm flung dry from years where I lay drowned.
Hours snap at my vanishing toes, lick
my footprints backing across the sand.
Watch—I'll wave with a dwindling hand:

a small child, safe in a final frame,
too young to know your name.

HARBOR

I catch myself drifting
toward you yet.
When I am tired, hours seem to be lifting
me into an old harbor. I forget

the tide is out now, foam breaking
on reefs. On black water, the hissing shelf
of the last wave shoreward, waking,
I catch myself.

THROUGH A PICTURE WINDOW

Westerns ride through the room, but she lies easy
in the greased blue light of pistols. He wears
the flat flash of a knife fight without blinking—
the cocked thumbs, the silences aren't theirs.
Swinging doors don't open upon their street
tonight. Other shadows drag in the dust down
somebody else's noon. They can trade glances
cool as beer, two strangers in a tough town.

DIAMOND

"She bid me take love easy,
as the leaves grow on the tree"
—W.B. Yeats
For my daughter Catherine at her wedding

This diamond was leaves
I am to take love lightly as
the silken shivering leaves
sift down from green to brown
as lightly as I am to take you
leaves sink deep in ground
turn black beneath the hills
turn carbon hard to coal
burn pale and wear to white
cold gemstone in the shale
so rock fall wears away
earth gives up diamond
so leaves come back to light
to shed a razor dust
to scar the face of steel
to split the very light to rainbow
splinters on the lancet edge
of leaves I take love lightly as.

EXPRESS FROM THE NORTH

For my son John at his wedding

Express from the north, do you hear it? roaring in
cold, enormous, storming this small station
to sweep the leaf crowd in the dawn din
to a timetable's ultimate destination.
Trees are sucked low by the rush of it,
dark blurs waving goodbye, goodbye
as green goes out. We have no ticket
saying we must leave with the season. Lie
warm with me, hear how the wind wails on,
diminished down the scale of the far hills.
We are left safe in a quietness the dawn
snow-sift, the small tick of the heart fills.

STAINED GLASS

From the day side you are pot-metal, no more
than crosshatch and stipple of dull planes
propped by iron bars to the downpour
punishment of the rains.
You are old wounds, bits of bubble and streak,
scabbed crust of lichen and heat grooves,
cobwebs, soldering, leads that leak—
but turn your face to me and the sun moves
by grace of your red scars; your blues lock
the sky in place, a shelter. I forget
in such light how the mullions crack and pock,
how north wind buckles the leads yet,
how your iron bleeds down the rock.

-IV-

ON NIGHTS LIKE THESE

OLD HOUSE

Our fingerprints are on every door, but slam one
and wallpaper bits may slide from the woodwork. Roses,
colonial views, Roman ruins, stars—they stare
from our distant walls. Somebody's buried garden
pushes up warped tulips under the porches.

Our children yell, "I'm home!" down the dark halls,
but a scent of coal climbs from the cellar yet
on damp days. Walls that seem smooth and bare
show, in a sidelong light, where a bookshelf was.
Here in our far-off bedroom, who knows where
somebody sits for someone yet, smiling,
her arms lifted, mirrored across this air?

A crack in a quarter-round will sometimes spit out
rusted pins, or a long, black, glistening hair.

SHELL STATIONS

Do you remember great shells
glowing at sundown—
how farmlands, gathering dark
in their windbreaks and barns, lit
those yellow cockles, hot
and fluted at crossroads?
  Slums, swamps,
whistle-stops, mountain shacks,
coal towns in black-running rain
raised clean shells over
our sleep. As if
there were dreams there
brighter than Venus, older,
more golden
than anything, even money.

PHAROS

The reefs are still there,
and shoals—ruinous, tide-ripped
graveyards. Greeks, aware
of what cannot be changed, charted theirs. Egypt
set priests at signal fires. Rome built towers,
wonders of the world, and where they were
stood later lights of ours
with salt-caked names: Haulbowline Rock, Barfleur,
Eddystone, Dhu Heartach, Cape Race,
Lizard, The Graves. Caissons were sunk
in muck, tons of rock joggled in place,
stones corbelled, a thousand fires shrunk
to a lone, revolving eye or a honed star
to slit distance, flicker: Beware. Beware.
But beacons wear away under sea stroke. Radar
speeds to us now through the howling air
with the same warning Greeks at their oars kept
time to: reefs and shoals wait where
they have always been, fanged, seething, wave-swept.

GETTING THE PICTURE

Holding her naked child, she squats
beyond words. Columns of newsprint
break ranks at her, go around.

She is young as old madonnas, foreign
like them, but her skin
is bone-tight, her bare feet wrung

tight to the tramped-down dirt
she seems to be trying to get into. She cries
something we can't hear; her

eyes glitter and her baby dangles
until her howl, life-size,
is a black hole eating outward like napalm, until

too close, she draws past, blows up. Words
are huge on the page, but machines have arranged
ink dots in a cloud where a woman was.

SAFETY PINS

They come from our factories in rows without expression.
Safety is their name, but holes are their trade,
                  and holding.
They will hold forever, if necessary,
while tears widen around them,
until metal glints from some obscure corner,
and there they lie in their rust, empty helmets
safely pinning ruin together.

TRICK OR TREAT

The ghost is a torn sheet,
the skeleton's suit came from a rack in a store
the witch is flameproof, but who knows
what dark streets they have taken here?
Brother Death, here is a candy bar.
For the lady wearing the hat from Salem: gum.
And a penny for each eye, Lost Soul.
They fade away with their heavy sacks.
Thanks! I yell just in time.

                              Thanks for another year!

THE DRINKERS

Dandelions suck tart juice from the ground
even in May, when they bloom with the greenish-yellow
color of sun after snow. Children taste that brown
bitterness, but they split the stems with their tongues
to make a wig of the dead-white, corkscrew ringlets,
or bring bouquets that are plump as the damp and downy
innocence of a chick, and stain your fingers—
strong drink from the ground. The flowers won't die.
Snap them off and they grow. As days pass,
they age to silvery heads. Seeds fly
on every wind from ripe skulls in the grass.

CASSANDRA AND THE DOUBLE-DECKED DOOM

My first English morning, too young to die,
I rocketed down the wrong side of the road
in a bus as red as blood and twice as high
as a scream—there was another swaying load
of Times readers hurtling down on us
from the wrong side of the road, too,

                          hell-for-leather.

"Fares!" called the conductor. Bus met bus,
missing by inches. Reading tomorrow's weather,
my seatmate nodded. Snored. As usual,
I was cursed with a day-long view of doom dawning
double-decked over the next hill,
and the rest of the world yawning.

SATURDAY MORNING IN CEDAR FALLS, IOWA

Parked cars catch Main Street
mirrored with its shop windows
against slipping sky, and passing cars
stream across glass with strolling
people, who never seem to reflect on

where they are. Only a light post
knows, perhaps, or blunt muzzles of trucks,
bottles behind that bar,
or a bone? They wait
to come down labeled: The Age of. The rest

grows thin where it is and slides by,
showing the sky through, smelling of fields
under the pavement's sweating tar, and only
one geranium on a high sill
says *Stop* with its red.

NAMING THE BONES

Neatly labeled, picked naked as stones,
he backed the children up with his strung bones,
dancing a bit. Holes where his eyes had been
stood ajar, horror crawled out and in,
so their mother had to step up to name in full
his metacarpals, scapula, clavicle,
shake his hand while pointing out with gravity
the greater and the lesser sigmoid cavity,
whirl him around like a bird cage, front to back,
give a swat to his sacroiliac
until, wrapped in his Greek and Latin shroud,
he made their dangling mandibles clack loud.
How they laughed as they rode their knotted white
spines and their straddling thigh bones out of sight
of his egg-shell grin at their strung bones
neatly labeled, picked naked as stones.

HIDEOUTS

Blankets. Beneath the bed.
Corners. The closet
with mother smells. Hiss
of tall grass in the wind.
Treehouse knotholes the whole
summer round. Secret codes.
Whispers. Clubhouses. Cars.
Clothes and dark glasses. Lies.
Hot and close love, and
habit's smooth skin.
Then nothing but
body ease. Quiet face.
Under tear-glaze
the eye's dark fly.

THE AERIALISTS

High-wire clowns catch us in cunning laughter.
X marks the spotlit aerie where they stare
down, teetering, crawling on all-fours after,
bicycling backward along the air.

Such bliss is painted upon their faces.
Like children pratfalling overhead,
they make nursery floors of high places.
Almost, almost we lose our dread…

Stripped of disguise,
sleek on a glittering thread,
their grace bows, riding our stunned applause,
and there's no net below. There never was.

-V-

THE PATH OF AN OLD AIR

THE REFUGEES

High over the chanting of the Mass
a man, woman and child are wandering
through thickets of stained glass.
He leads the donkey, hurrying
over stones. The child cries,
perhaps, held so tightly. They must go
through lines, cross borders, but angel eyes
track them, for each wears a halo
like a wreath of warm breath
in the cold country they pass through.
They will be sent back to Nazareth.
There is nothing we can do.

ROMAN ARCH AT ORANGE

One of those old doorways to nowhere,
foursquare, straddling the hot road.
Too huge to be circled, it waits there,
framing your destination in a bowed
black gap. You cannot choose but come
closer, dwarfed by that weathered arch
menacing, stonily useless, dumb.
If, brave as the Romans were, you march
under that monumental weight, you pass
thresholds worn as a wailing wall
to see shadowed before you on the grass
a monstrous, humpbacked victory. They call
these *arcs de triomphe,* and I think they are:
they fade so slowly on your backward view,
and roads branch from that victory like a star
once you pass through.

JUDY

The men are tin or straw,
but her face is real
with tears, and white as her bobby socks.
She wants to go back: that voice
cries from the screen once more, homeless—
a song's blue arch
greens, helpless as leaves, to the yellow
syrup of lemon drops.
She's going to see the Wizard again.
                              Stop her.
He died years ago, wealthy, in Oz.
She carries innocence off,
hugging it like her dog.

CHECKMATE

Only her king is left. She seethes with shame
as usual, yet must admire this game,
this ancient play that seems a pastime, still
trailing its old illusion of free will.
Alice traveled her chessboard in a train,
the clever child: Victorian rules were plain,
the moves prescribed, players all black or white,
no gray halfway, right wrong or wrongly right.

She's not their child. She knows why she has seen
stone chessboards carved on castles, checkered green
with lichen, coats of arms bearing a pawn:
old fighters sired her, rebels mated, gone,
who played the game as if the end weren't known
from the beginning, stood, a king alone
raging like her, at bay on black or red,
too proud to hear *shah mat*, the king is dead.

TO AN HISTORIAN

By sea light picture a skin diver
flippering the ooze of an ocean floor,
the prodigal returned, a sole survivor
thought drowned millenniums before.
He swims back out of the certain death
of unplumbed air, dazzle and thunder.
Strapped at his back he wears his chambered breath.
The frail shell of his skull crawls with a wonder.
Queer fish—see how he swims cold
to the lure of the maternal, circling sea,
for he's found two Greek amphorae from some old
beautiful world of his. Triumphantly,
he dives air-ward, leaving the sea behind
to grope for him at the shore's edge. Man is blind
to any past but the past he wants to find.

SARAH

If grief existed, heaps of dirty clothes
existed too. She wore grief smooth and thin
and docile as old linen. Worry rose
yeasty but useful, could be kneaded in
to serve her. She knew how to keep her dread
scoured to the bare board fact. Make do, make do
her gnarled hands told us, but those glittering eyes
she skewered life with—what was it they said?
I knew her old, threatened with deadly new
dangers of rest and peace. Without surprise,
she made good use of joy. When pleasure came,
she called it by its spare and proper name.

AN OLD WOMAN REMEMBERS

1. CHILDHOOD

We ran streaming
through pocked puddles, danced
naked with lightning.

Violence of a summer storm
played over us.

Dim with rain, we lay face down
where the sidewalk's gray rafts surfaced
holding the sun's heat, bits of leaves,
        snapped twigs,
and worms crawled up from drowning.

2. LOVE

Sometimes on chill mornings
clouds, mirrored thin gold,
swim in the light across
high windows, and children
shout, roller skating, the streets
fresh with their clean clashing.

Spring has not come, nothing
is green but light, growing, and yet
in a garden of sticks and straw
      a woman is smiling,
for her name has been said with a certain
inflection. Her eyes reflect what comes, cloudy.
She turns toward happiness, and begins.

3. CHILDBIRTH

When I was everything, everything but me took
(how could I have forgotten?)
one step back and left me
newborn at the eye of death, giving
my own cry as birds do, driven
from cover at the sound of a gun.
                    That scream
wakes me now. At the eye of a dark door
my child utters himself in terror.
(How could I have forgotten?)
Give him to me.
Milk flows for him in this enemy country.

EXHIBIT

She lies on her back behind glass,
signs on her jaw and thigh: Dental Caries,
Traces of Cloth Visible Here. She wears her gray
carefully-braided hair yet, and small hands
crossed under her chin. Bent double, toes spread,
mouth fallen open, she appears
to cry out, staring up.
   Small children ask,
   What is it?
   Older children mark the glass with their noses,
   hands, foreheads.
Earth-colored, doubled up,
she lies ready for birth, or childbirth.
A girl's glossy hair swings forward, that shape
darkening, for a moment, the pupils of her eyes.
   Parents read signs:
   She is old, yes, eight hundred years.
   A mummy. An old lady. An Indian.
   The showcase glow
   edges their bent faces; their edged voices
   move by every Saturday, Sunday, holiday—
   there are always crowds
   coming down corridors of dinosaur bones, fish
   fossils, stuffed birds and polar bears,
   ape skulls, to stop
where she lies with what is,
like a cry, coming from her.

THE CHURCHGOERS

In diamond air the snowy trees are bowed
before a sky so morning-glory blue
that della Robbia angels, two by two,
might pace its holy clarity like cloud.

The morning's an immaculate conception
where children walk on water turned to stars.
No path snakes through the garden. Nothing mars
this chaste and blue-veined pavement of perfection

that bears a child's weight, but to us is thin
as eggshell. Listen: a shining stave
of child song rings in the orchard's nave.
We sink at every step, blundering in.

GREENHOUSE

For Malcolm, my father, and David Malcolm, my son

Snow swarmed upon the blast.
Floundering, you and I
came to a house of glass
under a stony sky,
came to an August air
hung with the dense
odor of loam and mold
heavy as incense,
came to the fern frond,
tendril and petal curl
glowing in snow light,
came to the vulnerable
space where my memory
walled off one winter hour,
as glass will stand between
frost and a flower.

MORNING
For John

We find our way back, one by one
to the rising light and remembered voices,
one by one out of the dark
to a door we know, a pitcher of milk,
the bone-handled knife in the honey.

No one screams, holding me. No one
cries that the children are all here.
The table is set again for us.
I stand and stare at the clear water
falling, as promised, out of this tap.

-VI-

CONTEXTS

PROTEUS

I hang on to life but it changes shape
in my hands: the museum's bottled baby
dances until it's too perfect a wax copy
to be one, and it's real, a child
whose hooded eyes say nothing at all
is worth looking at, it isn't dancing
and yet I hang on until my son says
Come on, Mom, and see the Egyptians,
and we walk in our beautiful colored
flesh to the Egyptians, where life
blackens like bitumen, and shrinks
to paper on bone.
But I hang on

A clock's not time.
It only seems to be
because it moves.
Time, we think, moves.
   It runs in clocks.
We shape our clocks to fit
what we think must be there,
and then we ride it.
   We get to death on time.
When clocks stop, hang
empty upon the wall,
time is what goes on.

somehow to that dark brown crackle until, in the open air again, I see

it's neither wax nor flesh nor bone
but only something as manageable
as sunglasses and a car key

Bacilli have a contained look
drifting at random,
multiplying at night, perhaps,
sexlessly, to infiltrate dark files:
loveletters stained with rust,
small, vicious tears in perfect copies.

I find I'm holding too tight. I get
my fingers loose enough to see
I'll be looking through my fingerprints
for a while, and the key's
engraved on my palm.

WHAT IS

stands in silence: Iowa
an oak   morning
balancing on   cold
one foot,
lifting
in a star of arms
snow caught like light before
the arch of the red barn.
Poised in bronze,   Siva
waits
to
where a black bull   be
steams in the sun.   seen

SOMETHING

<pre>
is waited for at sundown   birds talk

in deep woods   against the dark

toadstools begin to be   aware   taking the sky away

        they let their outlines go   is this

                            now   all? they ask

            she feels them   among closing trees

        put on without moving   are you

        anticipation like smoke   there? they call

                trees deepen and listen   where?

                she is not what they hear

silence   air

is an absence the wind   thickens with buzzing dusk

plays at the

edge of   what comes

                spilling behind her like fog

        downhill through bushes?

                                    the path screams away

                            firelight beats about a clearing

                                she puts her back to it but

among

moths   her shadow opens a dark perspective back

the color of   where nothing is

old bones   coming from tree to tree now

    an owl   groping along her shadow's

    flattened on moonlight   grassy hall

            drops a mouse skull   whose

                wrapped in mouse-gray   door

                    gentle   she cannot

                        fur   find to close
</pre>

"LOVE IS NOT A SENTIMENT WORTHY OF RESPECT"

—Sido, mother of Colette

She has the glossy sheen of summer trees
setting their fruit in falling petals. Now
meadows translate themselves: the truth of bees
she's taken from a soft, abusing mouth,
and sings it to herself, a supple tune
that bends, not breaks the silence as she passes,
as faint an imprint as the woods of June
keep under springing fern, resilient grasses.

                        Come lie with you, but lie
                        lightly and then lie again, tell you
                        the fact that you exist
                        does not lie green and everywhere I go
                        like grass?

Even when sleep turns	Trees in a park, woman, dark
his body low	and snow.
He draws her out of her dark.	Through fingers snow branches
Waking, she flattens herself	slip fast things go. No
against what is	green limb fruit young sun
between them,	no soft small
gives off a bitterness	heavy sweet. Trees stand
like the taste of burning.	empty hand
	snow fall.

ROOMS IN THE GRASS

Children   have lived here   until
in   see how
the fall   rooms   winter
rake   are ruled in   and
dream   grass where   wind
houses in   someone   at
dead   dreamed them?   night
leaves.   come
They plan   thresholds   warm sun falls   through
              hearths   and
                niches for dishes   the house
              see?   little
              Here is where   by
              someone slept until   little
              everything   children dream   blows
                            of   away
                            shadows
                            of   Mesa
                            houses   Verde

                                            Pompeii

ABOUT THE AUTHOR

Nancy Price was born in Sioux Falls, South Dakota, the first child of Mary Day Price and Malcolm Price. She grew up in Detroit, Michigan, and in her early teens she saw her poems printed in *Scholastic Magazine,* and on the editorial page and the young writers' page of the *Detroit News.* She received her B.A. from Cornell College and her M.A. from the University of Northern Iowa, and studied at the Writers Workshop at the University of Iowa. Her husband, Howard Thompson, was a professor at U.N.I., and when their three children were in school, Nancy became a professor at U.N.I. also.

During the next years, more than one hundred of Nancy's poems and several of her short stories appeared in print. She was selected as a writer-in-residence at the Karolyi Foundation in Vence, France, the Tyrone Guthrie Centre in Ireland, and the Rockefeller Center on Lake Como in Italy, and received a writing fellowship from the National Endowment for the Arts.

Nancy's first novel was an historical novel of slavery in South Carolina: *A Natural Death*, published by Atlantic Monthly Press, Little, Brown. Her second, *An Accomplished Woman*, from Coward, McCann and Geoghegan, was a Book-of-the Month Club alternate and a New American Library paperback. *Sleeping With the Enemy*, her third novel, published by Simon and Schuster, became a Twentieth Century Fox feature film starring Julia Roberts. Her books have been translated into fifteen foreign languages.

Night Woman, Nancy's fourth novel, published by Pocket Books, was chosen by the Literary Guild, and was followed by three more novels, *Bonfire's Daughter, Snake in the Blackberries*, and *Two Liars and a Bride.* These last three novels, translated into French by Presses de la Cité in Paris, have gone from hardback to paperback editions and book club editions. The English manuscript of *Snake in the Blackberries*, retitled *No One Knows* and illustrated by Nancy, was published by Malmarie Press in Florida. Her seventh and eighth novels have been completed and are with her agent.

Nancy's husband died in 1995, and she lost her son John in 2005. She lives close to her other two children, Catherine and David, in Cedar Falls, Iowa, and spends her winters with her daughter-in-law and her family in Kissimmee, Florida. Her children have begged her to collect her poems from scattered newspapers and magazines, so for their sake she has brought out this, her newest illustrated book: *Two Voices and a Moon.*

NANCY PRICE

SELECTED BIBLIOGRAPHY

POETRY

The Aerialists. THE REPORTER, March 28, 1963.

An Old Woman Remembers. THE BLUE GUITAR, 1989.

The Bear. THE NEW YORK TIMES, July 6, 1965.

The Bell. LADIES' HOME JOURNAL, December 1966.

Books. THE HORN BOOK MAGAZINE, February 1966.

Breakers. THE NEW YORK TIMES, July 29, 1970.

The Cardinals. AMERICA, February 19, 1966.

Cassandra and the Double-decked Doom. THE ATLANTIC, May 1963.

Centennial of Shiloh. MIDWEST, Spring 1964.

Checkmate. THE NEW YORK TIMES, December 23, 1963.

Children On the Swings. THE NEW YORK TIMES, September 3, 1966.

Christmas Letter To a Friend On Mars. THE REPORTER, December 15, 1966.

The Churchgoers. COMMONWEAL, February 21, 1964.

City Child. THE COLORADO QUARTERLY, Autumn 1964.

The Climber. THE NEW YORK TIMES, January 11, 1968.

The Common Emperor. COMMONWEAL, May 14, 1965.

Corn. AMERICA, July 20, 1968.

Cornered Eye. AUDIENCE, Spring 1963.

Corn Field. KANSAS QUARTERLY, Spring 1970.

Day Lily. COMMONWEAL, October 27, 1967.

Daylily. TODAY, March 1967.

Diamond. QUARTERLY REVIEW OF LITERATURE, Winter 1970-71.

A Do-it-yourself Poem. POETRY NORTHWEST, Spring 1970.

The Dowagers d'Oro. HARPER'S BAZAAR, April 1964.

The Drinkers. THE NATION, October 23, 1967.

Duet. AMERICA, April 19, 1973.

Eclipse. KAYAK, January 1968.

Eclipse of the Sun. TODAY, March 1967.

Exercise. THE CHRISTIAN SCIENCE MONITOR, March 28, 1963.

Exhibit. THE BLUE GUITAR, 1989.

Express From the North. AMERICA, October 29, 1966.

Flight. THE REPORTER, December 15, 1966.

Getting the Picture. THE NATION, November 11, 1968.

Greenhouse. COMMONWEAL, August 19, 1966.

The Grinder. THE NEW YORK TIMES, January 10, 1966.

Guitar. QUARTERLY REVIEW OF LITERATURE, Winter 1970-71.

Hackberry. THE NATION, November 10, 1969.

Harbor. KANSAS QUARTERLY, Winter 1970-71.

Hideouts. KAYAK, January 1968.

Home Movie. THE COLORADO QUARTERLY, Autumn 1964.

How Do You Tell An Arrowhead From A Stone? KAYAK, January 1968.

In Cooling Love Like Air. LADIES' HOME JOURNAL, November 1965.

Intersection. THE REPORTER, April 7, 1966.

In the Water World. THE NEW YORK TIMES, June 4, 1966.

In This Same Country. AMERICA, December 24-31, 1966.

Keepsake (Tintype). COMMONWEAL, January 8, 1971.

Kensington Church Street, London. McCALL's, August 1967.

The Knife Thrower. McCALL's, September 1967.

Landmark (The Cup). THE NATION, May 2, 1966.

Look, See the Cat. THE NEW YORK TIMES, February 24, 1964.

"Love Is Not A Sentiment Worthy of Respect." SHENANDOAH, Autumn 1969.

Man and Dog. KANSAS QUARTERLY, Winter 1968.

Maple Fools, Miser Oaks. THE ATLANTIC, October 1966.

Midstream. COMMONWEAL, September 26, 1969.

Milk and Honey. BELOIT POETRY JOURNAL, Spring 1963.

Milkweed. COMMONWEAL, March 24, 1967.

Morning (Seven A.M.). AMERICA, October 5, 1968.

Naming the Bones. THE REPORTER, May 20, 1965.

Nassau and Back: Casino, Grand Bahama. KANSAS QUARTERLY, Winter 1971-2.

A Needle. KAYAK, Spring 1970.

Night Train. THE MIDWEST QUARTERLY, Summer 1969.

Old House. THE QUARTERLY REVIEW OF LITERATURE, Winter 1970-71.

Oliver Wendell Holmes. THE NEW YORK TIMES, October 3, 1963.

On a Globe Turning. AMERICA, May 23, 1970.

One-night Fair. COMMONWEAL, February 25, 1966.

Othello. HARPER'S BAZAAR, April 1964.

Out of Love: The Break. QUARTERLY REVIEW OF LITERATURE, Winter 1970-71.

Passing Through. THE NEW YORK TIMES, February 23, 1969.

Pharos. THE REPORTER, January 27, 1966.

Preserves. KANSAS QUARTERLY, Winter 1968.

Proteus. QUARTERLY REVIEW OF LITERATURE, Winter 1970-71.

Roman Arch At Orange. THE NEW YORK TIMES, August 3, 1964.

The Refugees. AMERICA, December 20, 1969.

Safety Pins. KAYAK, Spring 1970.

Sandal. THE REPORTER, June 16, 1966.

Sarah. COMMONWEAL, December 4, 1964.

Scissors. KAYAK, January 1968.

Something. KAYAK, Spring 1969.

Soursop. SATURDAY REVIEW, May 7, 1966.

Sparklers. TODAY, March 1967.

The Spinner. NORTHWEST REVIEW, Fall-Winter 1967-68.

The Squirrel. THE HORN BOOK MAGAZINE, October 1967.

Stained Glass. SATURDAY REVIEW, October 24, 1964.

Street. THE REPORTER, March 9, 1967.

The Sum of Christmas. McCALL's, December 1963.

The Ten-toed Signature. THE ATLANTIC, February 1965.

Tides. THE REPORTER, March 9, 1967.

To An Historian. THE NEW YORK TIMES, April 14, 1964.

Trick Or Treat. THE ATLANTIC, November 1967.

The Umbrella. THE COLORADO QUARTERLY, Autumn 1964.

Ventriloquist's Wife. SHENANDOAH, Summer 1967.

Villanelle. THE NEW YORK TIMES, December 14, 1969.

What Is. KAYAK, Spring 1969.

Woman With Mango, KANSAS MAGAZINE, Winter 1967-68.

Word-eater. ETC., December 1966.

Year After Year (What Spring Is For). CHILDREN OF THE MOON,
    Spring 1973.

Note: The title of a poem as originally published
is given in parenthesis.

BOOKS IN WHICH POEMS HAVE BEEN REPRINTED

MODERN POETS, BRITISH AND AMERICAN, Pflaum, 1966.

THE NEW YORK TIMES BOOK OF VERSE, Macmillan, 1970.

THE DIAMOND ANTHOLOGY, Poetry Society of America, A. S. Barnes, 1971.

ANTHOLOGY, Poetry Society of Georgia, 1972.

BELIEVE AND MAKE-BELIEVE, Allyn and Bacon, 1973.

INTERPRETING LITERATURE, Holt, Rinehart and Winston, editions 1965-1974.

A CELEBRATION OF CATS, Paul S. Eriksson, 1974.

OUT OF THIS WORLD, POEMS FROM THE HAWKEYE STATE, Iowa State University Press, 1975.

I HEAR MY SISTERS SAYING, Crowell, 1976.

SHORT STORY PUBLICATION

"The Invisible Ones." (Later used in the novel SLEEPING WITH THE ENEMY.) VIRGINIA QUARTERLY REVIEW, Winter 1968.

"White Mouse." (Later used in the novel SLEEPING WITH THE ENEMY.) VIRGINIA QUARTERLY REVIEW, Winter 1969.

"The Woman Who Never Was." GOOD HOUSEKEEPING (London edition), July 14, 1988.

During 1983 to 1985 the PEN Syndicated Fiction Project selected three of Nancy Price's short stories to be illustrated and printed in newspaper magazine sections.

1. "They Don't Listen." (Later used in the novel SLEEPING WITH THE ENEMY.)

    CHICAGO TRIBUNE "Book World," September 11, 1983.

    HARTFORD COURANT "Northeast Magazine," October 23, 1983.

    KANSAS CITY STAR, September 11, 1983.

    MIAMI HERALD "Tropic Magazine," September 25, 1983.

    MINNEAPOLIS STAR & TRIBUNE "Picture," September 25, 1983.

    NEWSDAY, September 18, 1983.

    THE OREGONIAN "Northwest Magazine," September 25. 1983.

ROCKY MOUNTAIN NEWS, September 25, 1983.

SAN FRANCISCO CHRONICLE "This World," September 11, 1983.

KANSAS CITY STAR, September 25, 1983. Also printed in the book, THE AVAILABLE PRESS/PEN SHORT STORY COLLECTION, Ballantine 1985.

2. "The Trucker and the Mermaid."

CHICAGO TRIBUNE "Book World," January 1, 1984.

MINNEAPOLIS STAR AND TRIBUNE "Picture," January 9, 1984.

3. "Cover Girl."

NEWSDAY, September 1985.

"Booklands," a serial story in eighteen parts, each illustrated by the author. (A young people's version of the first section of Nancy Price's novel, NO ONE KNOWS). THE COURIER, Waterloo, Iowa, October 17- November 25, 2005.

BOOK PUBLICATION
UNITED STATES EDITIONS

A NATURAL DEATH (hardback). An Atlantic Monthly Press Book. Little, Brown and Company, Boston 1973.

AN ACCOMPLISHED WOMAN (hardback). Coward, McCann and Geoghegan, New York 1979.

AN ACCOMPLISHED WOMAN (paperback). New American Library, New York 1979.

SLEEPING WITH THE ENEMY (hardback). Simon and Schuster, New York 1987.

SLEEPING WITH THE ENEMY (paperback). Jove Books, New York 1988.

SLEEPING WITH THE ENEMY (paperback movie edition). Berkeley, New York 1991.

NIGHT WOMAN (hardback). Pocket Books, Simon and Schuster, New York 1992.

NIGHT WOMAN (paperback). Pocket Star Books, Simon and Schuster, New York 1993.

NO ONE KNOWS (hardback). Malmarie Press, Florida 2004. (Published first in French by Presses de la Cité, Paris, 2000, titled SNAKE IN THE BLACKBERRIES.)

Foreign Editions: AN ACCOMPLISHED WOMAN

KOBIETA SPELNIONA (paperback, Poland). Amber, Warsaw 1995.

Foreign Editions: SLEEPING WITH THE ENEMY

SLEEPING WITH THE ENEMY (hardback, *England, Australia, New Zealand, South Africa)*. Century Hutchinson, London 1987.

SLEEPING WITH THE ENEMY (paperback, *England*). Arrow Books 1988, 1991.

TIL DODEN OSS SKILLER (hardback, *Norway)*. Damm 1987.

LA COLOMBE NOIRE (hardback, *France*). Bookclub France Loisirs, Presses de la Cité, Paris 1988.

LA COLOMBE NOIRE (paperback, *France)*. Presses de la Cité, Paris 1988.

LES NUITS AVEC MON ENNEMI (paperback, *France*). Presses de la Cité, Paris 1988. (Note: same book also appeared with another cover showing Julia Roberts.)

SOVA HOS FIENDEN (hardback, *Sweden*). Forum, Stockholm 1988.

DORMINDO COM O INIMIGO (paperback, *Brazil*). Editora Best Seller, Sao Paulo 1988.

O INIMIGO DORME AO LADO (paperback, *Brazil*). Editora Best Seller, Sao Paulo 1988.

IO TI LASCERO (hardback, *Italy*). Rizzoli, Milan 1988.

IO TI LASCERO *(*hardback, *Italy*). Euroclub, Rizzoli 1989.

DORMIR CON EL ENEMIGO (paperback, *Argentina*). Emece Editores, Buenos Aires 1989.

FATALE ONTMOETING (hardback, *Netherlands*). Uitgeverij Kadmos, Weert 1990.

IN DE STILTE VAN DE NACHT (hardback, *Netherlands*). Zuid-Hollandsche 1992.

SCHREIE IN DER NACHT (paperback, *Germany*). Bastei Lubbe, Bremen 1990.

SLEEPING WITH THE ENEMY (hardback, *Israel. Hebrew*). Ma'ariv
Book Guild, Tel Aviv, publisher E. Lewin-Epstein, Ltd., Bat-Yam 1990.

SYPIAJAC Z WROGIEM (paperback, *Poland*). Wydawnictwo Amber,
Warsaw 1992.

DURMIENDO CON SU ENEMIGO (hardback, *Spain*).
CirculodeLectores, S.A., Barcelona 1993.

DURMIENDO CON SU ENEMIGO (paperback, *Spain*). Plaza & Janes,
Barcelona 1993.

DURMIENDO CON SU ENEMIGO (hardback, movie edition, *Spain*).
Novellas de Cine, Orbi Fabri, Barcelona 1995.

I SENG MED FJENDEN (paperback, *Denmark*). Asschenfeldt's Bogklub,
Copenhagen.

SLEEPING WITH THE ENEMY (paperback, *Japan*). Tokyo.

Foreign Editions: NIGHT WOMAN

NIGHT WOMAN (paperback, *England*). Fontana, HarperCollins, London
1993.

NIGHT WOMAN (hardback, *Russia*). Gustav Meyrink, Moscow 1994.

DIE FRAU IM SCHATTEN (paperback, *Germany*). Bastei Lubbe,
Bremen 1993.

MUJER DE LA NOCHE (paperback, *Argentina*). Emece Editores, Buenos
Aires 1994.

KLAMSTVO Z LASKY (paperback, *Czechoslovakia*). Ikar 1994.

ZENA NOCIA (hardback, *Czechoslovakia*). Ikar 1994.

NIGHTWOMAN (paperback, *Korea*). Shin Won, Seoul 1994.

NATTENS KVINNE (hardback, *Norway*). Hjemmets Bokforlag, Oslo
1994.

LA DAME DE LA NUIT (hardback, *France*). Club France Loisirs, Presses
de la Cité, Paris 1994.

LA DAME DE LA NUIT (paperback, *France*). Presses de la Cité, Paris
1994.

LA DONNA DAI DUE VOLTI (paperback, *Italy*). Pandora, Sperling &
Kupfer, Milan 1995.

LA DONNA DAI DUE VOLTI (hardback, *Italy*). Euroclub, Sperling &
Kupfer, Milan 1995.

LA DONNA DAI DUE VOLTI (paperback, *Italy*). Speerling & Kupfer, Milan 1998.

NATTKVINNAN (hardback, *Sweden*). Forum, Stockholm 1993.

NOCE MARY ELIOT (paperback, *Poland*). Amber, Warsaw 1995.

NIGHT WOMAN (paperback, *Japan*). Mystery Paperbacks, Tokyo.

Foreign editions: BONFIRE'S DAUGHTER

L'INCENDIAIRE (hardback, *France*). Presses de la Cité, Paris 1998.

L'INCENDIAIRE (hardback, *France*). Club France Loisirs, Paris 1998.

L'INCENDIAIRE (paperback, *France*). Presses de la Cité. Paris 1999.

L'INCENDIAIRE (paperback, *Canada*). Presses Solar Belfond 1999.

Foreign Editions: SNAKE IN THE BLACKBERRIES

UN ÉCART DE JEUNESSE (hardback, *France*). Presses de la Cité, Paris 2000.

UN ÉCART DE JEUNESSE (paperback, *France*). Presses de la Cité, Paris 2001.

(The English language edition of SNAKE IN THE BLACKBERRIES was later published by the Malmarie Press, Florida in 2004, entitled NO ONE KNOWS.)

Foreign Editions: TWO LIARS AND A BRIDE

L'ENFANT DU MENSONGE (hardback, *France*). Presses de la Cité, Paris 2003.

L'ENFANT DU MENSONGE (paperback, *France*). Presses de la Cité, Paris 2005.

Note: The drawing for the introductory page to section II of TWO VOICES AND A MOON was copied by the author from the original fourteenth century English stained glass in the Victoria and Albert Museum, London.

The drawing for the introductory page to section V is from fourteenth century stained glass in the cathedral at Orvieto, Italy.

INDEX OF TITLES

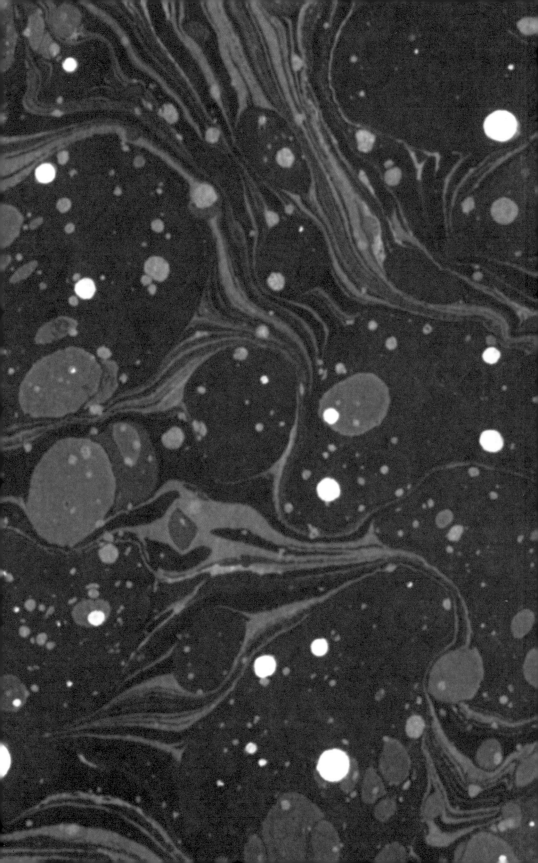